NIGHT ANIMALS

NIGHT ANIMALS

by MILLICENT E. SELSAM

SCHOLASTIC BOOK SERVICES

NEW YORK • TORONTO • LONDON • AUCKLAND • SYDNEY • TOKYO

Photo credits:

Cover, 22: Karl H. Maslowski/Photo Researchers; 9 Sdeuard C. Bisserot/ Bruce Coleman; 10 Leonard Lee Rue III/Bruce Coleman; 13 Harry Rogers/Photo Researchers; 14 Leonard Lee Rue III/Design Photographer International; 16 Leonard Lee Rue III/Bruce Coleman; 17 Ed Cesar/ National Audubon Society/Photo Researchers; 18-19 Sdeuard C. Bisserot/Bruce Coleman; 20 New York Zoological Society Photo; 21 The American Museum of Natural History; 24 Karl H. Maslowski/Photo Researchers; 25 Wilford L. Miller/Photo Researchers; 27 Alexander Lowry/Photo Researchers; 28 The American Museum of Natural History; 30-31 Photo Researchers; 33 Sdeuard C. Bisserot/Bruce Coleman; 34 The American Museum of Natural History; 35 Karl H. Maslowski/ Photo Researchers; 36, backcover H. Charles Laun/Photo Researchers; 38 The American Museum of Natural History; 40 Alan A. Geiger.

ISBN 0-590-30058-X

Copyright © 1979 by Millicent E. Selsam. All rights reserved. Published by Scholastic Book Services, a division of Scholastic Magazines, Inc.

12 11 10 9 8 7 6 5 4 3 2 1   9   9/7 0 1 2 3 4/8

Printed in the U.S.A.   18

For
Miwa, Alan and Kazumi

It is nightime.
You are sleeping in your bed.
Many of the animals outside are sleeping too.
But others are stirring.
Let's see who is awake.

A little mouse steps softly
out of its grassy nest.
It is time to look for seeds, or berries,
or nuts to nibble on.

But someone in the dark forest
heard the tiny sounds the mouse made.
Suddenly a shadow swoops down.
It is the screech owl.
It closes its wings as it lands,
ready to dig its hooked claws into the mouse.
But the mouse is gone.
It ran back into its nest.

A big bullfrog is sitting in the pond.
Its eyes seem to pop out of its head.
If any small animal moves near,
the frog's tongue will flash out.
The animal will tumble into the frog's mouth.

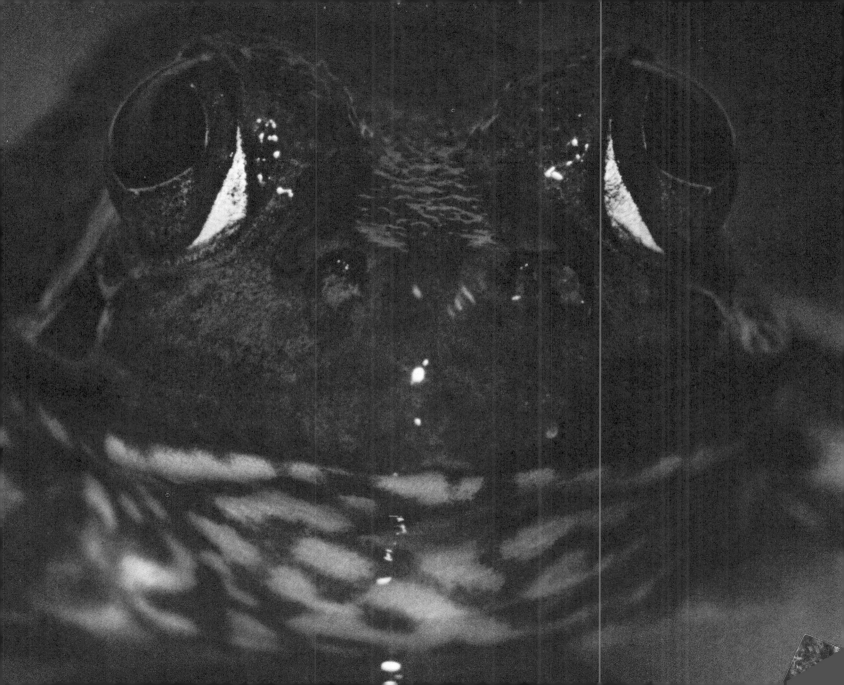

A quiet movement among the trees
makes you turn your head.
A deer is standing there.
It lifts its thin legs high
as it walks over to an oak tree
and nibbles on the twigs.

The flying squirrel sitting in the moonlight
looks like any other squirrel. But wait.
It has a flap of skin
connecting its front and back legs.

When it shoves off from the branch of a tree,
it stretches out its legs,
and glides 150 feet through the air.

The luna moth has just come out of its cocoon
and spread her pale green wings.
Soon she will give off a powerful odor
into the night air.
Then a male luna moth will fly to her
from more than five miles away.
They will mate and the female luna
will then fly around and deposit her eggs
on the leaves of oak, willow, beech,
and hickory trees.

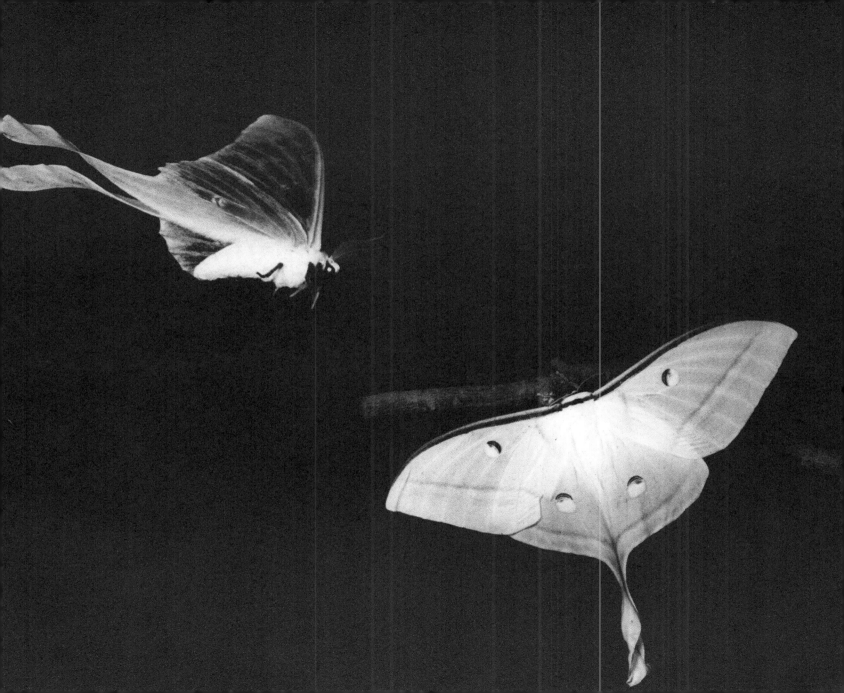

The baby opossums are crawling
all over their mother.
Soon she will shove them off
and find something for them to eat.

Maybe the wild cherries are ripe.
Or perhaps the blackberries have turned juicy.
If not, she can probably find a mouse
or some worms.
Almost anything will do.

Five baby barn owls are sitting in the corner
of an old barn.
They are making clicking noises
to show they are hungry.
The mother barn owl has to feed
these baby birds for eight weeks.
Then they, too, will leave the barn at night
to find their own food.

The gray fox was hunting for food in the forest.
Now he is taking a rest.

Meanwhile the red fox went to the fields
at the edge of the forest.
See what it caught!

Five black masks and five pairs of yellow eyes
shine in the moonlight.
Five young racoons are out looking for food.
They are on the way to a small pool
where they will fish for crayfish and frogs.

Beavers are busy cutting down trees
all through the night.
This one is chewing on the bark of a young tree.

And this one has its teeth around a tree trunk.
It will gnaw its way through
until the tree falls.

The tiny lights of fireflies are twinkling on and off.
Fireflies are not really flies. They are beetles.
There are many different kinds of fireflies.
Each kind of firefly has its own signal—
its own special way of flashing its lights.

A female firefly sits at the tip
of a blade of grass.
A male firefly flies around her
flashing his lights.
If it is the right signal,
the female will flash back
and the male will land beside her.

There are thousands of insects in the air
above the lake.
In one night a bat can eat hundreds of them.
This bat is skimming above the water
picking up insects.
Every once in a while it will swoop down
onto the lake
and take a sip of water.

There are baby rabbits in this nest.
A quick movement — what was that?

As mother rabbit turns to look,
a weasel slips away.
It has a mouse in its mouth.
The baby rabbits are safe for awhile.

The porcupine is sitting in a pine tree.
Its quills look like a bundle of pine needles.
The sweet smell of raspberries
reaches its nose.
Now the porcupine will back down the trunk
and waddle over to the bushes
where the berries are ripe.
There it will feast until its belly is full.

A mother skunk and her three babies
are taking a walk in the forest.
As she goes along, the mother skunk
turns up stones
and digs into rotten stumps.
Maybe juicy caterpillars and worms
are hiding there.
She may also catch a mouse
or a cricket on the forest floor.
There she will share the food
with her young ones.

A pale light appears in the sky.
Night is over.
The foxes will go back to their dens.
The beavers will go back to their lodges.
The racoons will go back to their holes in a tree.
The bats will go back
to their caves or hollow trees
and hang upside down.
The porcupine will climb up a tall tree
and stretch out between two big branches.

All the other animals of the night will find
a place to rest during the day.
Then the sun will come up.
The day animals will start to wake up.
You too.